ORGANIC GARDENING

A Guide for Beginners

by

Ruth Jacobs

This book will enable the reader to make a start at gardening using natural materials.

Each page deals with a different topic, so just look up the subject which interests you.

For further information, a selection of books is listed at the back.

Alfresco Books

ISBN 1 873727 14 3

British Library Cataloguing in Publication Data. A catalogue record for this book is available from the British Library.

First published in March 1996 by *Alfresco Books*
Second, revised and enlarged edition, August 1999
7 Pineways, Appleton, Warrington, Cheshire, WA4 5EJ
Telephone/Fax: 01925 267503

Publisher's Note: While every effort has been made to ensure that the information given in this book is correct the Publisher does not accept responsibility for any inaccuracy.

Cover - Gordon Firth

Line drawings - Jackie Woolsey

Typeset and design - Jen Darling

Production - MFP Design & Print

FOREWORD

Ruth Jacobs has long been a supporter of organic gardening and the work of the HDRA, so I was delighted to be asked to write the Foreword to this book.

There has never been a greater demand for information about organic gardening. Every time a pesticide is banned, or a new food scare erupts, more people contact us at HDRA for practical advice on environmentally friendly gardening. Whether it's growing food, a lawn or an ornamental border — on a large scale or in a tiny back yard — people want to do it without using chemicals.

But many people who want to take this step are unsure about what to do, what not to do and where to start. This is where a good basic book, in simple format, easy to access, that doesn't get bogged down in excess detail, is invaluable.

Organic Gardening (A Guide for Beginners) opens the door of organic gardening to newcomers, while reminding 'old hands' of the value, and desirability, of organic principles and practices. Ruth has pulled together all the many strands that organic gardeners rely on and produced a book to instil enthusiasm and energy into everyone who reads it.

Alan Gear, Chief Executive, HDRA

CONTENTS

Part 4: FIGHTING PESTS AND DISEASES

Part 5: ORGANIC EXTRA

A SIMPLE CONVERSION CHART

This is to help those who prefer to use imperial measures. All the measurements given here are approximate.

2.5 cms	=	1 inch
5 cms	=	2 inches
10 cms	=	4 inches
30 cms	=	1 foot
50 grams	=	1.75 ounces
100 grams	=	3.5 ounces
150 grams	=	5.25 ounces
200 grams	=	7 ounces
1 litre	=	1.75 pints
4.5 litres	=	1 gallon

Part One

WHY ORGANIC?

SOME COMMON QUESTIONS ANSWERED?

Q   Does organic gardening mean just not using chemicals?

A   That's only the tip of the iceberg; there's a lot more to it.

Q   What does the word organic mean?

A   Anything that has been alive, either animal or vegetable. If it is mineral it is not (biologically) organic.

Q   Does that mean that organic gardeners never use minerals?

A   No. Organic gardeners *do* use some minerals as well but only naturally occurring ones.

Q   So why do they call it organic gardening?

A   It *is* confusing. A better name would be biological gardening.

Q   Why are organic vegetables better?

A   Organically grown plants are stronger and more disease-resistant; they contain more vitamins and minerals and don't absorb heavy metals from polluted soil in the same way that chemically grown plants do.

Q   Surely it's all right to use chemical fertilisers as long as we also use some organic material?

A   Page 10 explains the arguments against.

Q   Why do people use chemicals if organic methods are better?

A   The chemical industry spends vast sums on advertising; no-one advertises manure!

Q   How do you manage pests and diseases without chemicals?

A   By understanding a plant's needs and its enemies' habits.

The following pages should help towards this understanding.

WHAT IS ORGANIC GARDENING?

- Organic growing means using no artificial fertilisers or chemical pesticides - it's a wholefood system. Only organic materials plus natural minerals are used.

- This way of growing respects the environment and is non-polluting. Modern methods destroy the natural world.

- Traditional gardening methods are combined with the most up-to-date techniques.

- It is also called biological or ecological gardening because only natural processes of recycling are used.

- It means feeding the soil, not the plant. Nature has designed plants to find their own food; they do it much better than we can.

- Organic growing is sustainable growing - a system that works indefinitely with a minimum of outside aid.

- It is vitally important to work with nature, not against. Nature ALWAYS wins any confrontation, as we know to our cost - ozone damage, poisoned seas, acid rain and the rest.

- Never forget that the soil is alive and that life must be cherished and preserved. This is the basic principle of organic growing.

- Preserving the balance of nature is an integral part of an organic system. We NEED the natural world: insects, flowers and wildlife.

- Organic gardening is conservation gardening.

WHAT'S WRONG WITH ARTIFICIAL FERTILISERS?

- Feeding plants pure chemicals is unnatural; it is force-feeding, intensive care. Organic growing uses only natural substances.

- As chemicals are not a wholefood, the plant is deprived of many minerals and other substances needed for full health.

- Adding pure minerals causes an imbalance in the soil, making some elements unavailable to the plant: for example, too much potash deprives the plant of magnesium.

- Anyone eating such plants, either animal or human, could suffer from mineral deficiency. It is well known that the modern diet is lacking in essential minerals.

- Organic matter helps to filter heavy metals from the soil; plants chemically-fed will absorb cadmium rather than zinc, for instance.

- Chemical fertilisers encourage surface rooting at the expense of deep roots, making the plant susceptible to drought, floods and bad weather conditions.

- Chemicals usually mean overfeeding, leading to soft sappy growth which is mainly water and attracts pests.

- The surplus nitrates pollute drinking water and kill fish.

- Chemical fertilisers discourage the living organisms in the soil, sometimes killing them.

- Chemical fertilisers contain no humus, an essential component of soil. Without humus the soil slowly dies.

- Chemical farming is responsible for droughts in many parts of the world and for the USA dustbowl, where nothing grows.

PESTICIDES CAN DAMAGE YOUR HEALTH

- These include fungicides, herbicides, weed killers, insecticides; all are biocides (life killers).

- Many are man-made inventions, similar to plastic or nylon and, like them, never rot down. They are here for good, in the air we breathe and the water we drink.

- Pesticide residues are in all our food and some of them are suspected of causing cancer, birth defects or genetic mutations, and other serious health problems over the long term.

- In the short term, handling chemicals may be even more dangerous; chemicals absorbed through the skin or inhaled can be lethal.

- So, they are a health hazard, both in the short and long term.

- Every year one or two are withdrawn from use, finally admitted to be dangerous. Which ones will be next?

- All the various chemicals combine to form a lethal, chemical cocktail, the effect of which is as yet unknown.

- They are passed down to babies in mothers' milk.

- Some biocides banned in the West are still being exported to the Third World, where thousands of people who handle them are poisoned every year.

- Much imported food contains British-made pesticide residues. So, despite the ban, we're still getting them!

- Do not be fobbed off with talk of 'insignificant amounts'. Our bodies are able to respond to minute quantities and an alien substance is still an intruder, no matter how small, and especially when taken regularly.

PESTICIDES AND THE ENVIRONMENT

- Pesticides kill not only the pest but its enemies too. Pests are much more resilient - result - a pest population explosion.

- In time pests develop resistance to chemicals, so that more powerful pesticides have to be developed. The malaria mosquito, for instance, is now resistant to almost every known chemical.

- Some newer pesticides are aimed specifically at one pest, or are advertised as 'safer' because they deactivate in the soil, but their residues are just as deadly and long-lasting.

- Farm weedkillers have killed 95% of English wild flowers. These so-called weeds are vital to provide habitats for friendly predators.

- As wild plants die, so does wildlife. A nesting pair of blue tits needs 15,000 caterpillars to rear a brood of young birds. No host plants? No blue tits.

- Poisoned insects and slugs are eaten by hedgehogs and other creatures. So poisons travel up the food chain, killing all the way. This nearly lost us all our golden eagles.

- Pesticides are polluting rivers and streams.

- They are present in all animals, including humans, and DDT is even present in Antarctic penguins.

- Sprayers are not accurately calibrated, so that droplets are floating in the air and being inhaled by us all.

- Pesticides interfere with the balance of nature, which normally prevents any one creature from becoming a nuisance. This is why slugs are such a problem; civilisation has removed many of their natural enemies.

- Pesticides kill not only the living creatures in the soil but the soil itself. If the soil dies, nothing will grow.

Part Two

ESSENTIAL BASIC KNOWLEDGE

WHAT IS SOIL?

- Plants will only thrive if the soil is healthy, so it's important to know something about the soil.

- Soil is the most important part of the garden: it has taken hundreds of years to build it up from the remains of plants, animals and ground-up rocks.

- Fertile soil containing plenty of organic matter is said to be in good heart, with a complete range of minerals, vitamins, proteins and other substances needed for plant health, as well as ample humus.

- A teaspoonful of soil contains literally millions of bacteria and fungi — micro-organisms, which need humus to stay alive.

- The only source of humus is organic matter, for example manure and compost, so regular applications are essential. There is no artificial or chemical substitute.

- Humus gives the soil structure, providing aeration and drainage, preventing waterlogging and anchoring the plants firmly.

- If no organic matter is added to the soil it slowly deteriorates and dies, becoming dry dust that blows or washes away - soil erosion.

- Once the soil is dead, nothing will grow in it, unless fed artificially.

- Peat, and its substitutes, are used in order to provide humus — a very inferior substitute for the real thing.

WHAT LIVES IN THE SOIL?

- Healthy soil is teeming with life - insects, worms, slugs, plus millions of micro-organisms - bacteria and fungi.

- They all play a part in recycling organic material into food for the next generation of plants.

- Possibly the most important are the bacteria and fungi, all of which do a different job.

- Some bacteria work the nitrogen cycle, whereby they convert atmospheric nitrogen into nitrates, the basic plant food.

- Others decompose dead organic matter back again into free-floating nitrogen.

- Yet other microbes help to feed the plant, in a mysterious process in which the plant roots signal that food is needed.

- This is a typical example of the interdependence of all living things, plant and animal. We all need each other.

- The plant cannot obtain food unless it has the co-operation of these organisms, which is why nothing will grow in dead soil. Try sowing seeds after a bonfire!

- Bacterial activity is dependent on the soil being warm enough and having the correct acid/alkali balance.

- Because bacteria can't work in the cold, organic plants sometimes take longer to get started, but they soon catch up.

- Earthworms play a vital part in keeping the soil healthy; their tunnels loosen and aerate the soil; they improve the structure and help to produce humus. Healthy soil will contain lots of worms.

HOW PLANTS FEED NATURALLY

- We don't need to feed plants; they feed themselves.

- But we do need to understand how they obtain their food.

- Plants feed in two ways - through their leaves and their roots.

- The leaves use carbon dioxide from the air to make growth, giving out oxygen in its place. This is called photosynthesis.

- This only happens in the light. Without light a plant dies.

- Plants also need minerals and other substances, usually taking them up through their lower roots.

- The plant selects which mineral it wants and only takes the amount it needs, when it needs it.

- Organic minerals, unlike the chemical sort, remain in the soil until needed, releasing their goodness very slowly so that over-feeding or imbalance is rare.

- Shallow surface roots are used by the plant to absorb water. Any chemical fertilisers added to the soil will dissolve into this water.

- In this way chemical fertilisers are absorbed by the plant immediately, causing a massive imbalance of minerals, while any surplus is leached away through the soil.

- Plants can also absorb some minerals through their leaves, either from the air or from a liquid feed.

- On the next page you will find details of the minerals and elements that the plant needs.

MINERAL REQUIREMENTS

- Plants need a number of minerals, all of which are present naturally in fertile, organic soil.

- The most important minerals are nitrates, phosphates and potash, commonly known by their chemical symbols N, P, K.

- Nitrates (or nitrogen) feed the green, leafy part of the plant; phosphates (or phosphorus) build up the root system; potash (or potassium) contributes to fruit and flower development.

- Three other elements are needed in smaller quantities - calcium, magnesium and sulphur.

- Then there are the trace elements which are needed in tiny amounts; the main ones are boron, manganese, iron, copper, zinc and molybdenum, plus several others.

- A shortage of any of these may lead to serious deficiency, disease or even the death of the plant.

- On the other hand, the plant may show no symptoms at all, but the animals and humans eating them could suffer as a result.

- Chemical fertilisers usually contain only a very limited range of minerals, so that the plants often lack very important elements.

- It is now realised that today's modern diet is seriously deficient in minerals, such as zinc and magnesium, which are essential for the healthy development of both the nervous system and the brain.

MINERALS FOR LIFE

All plants — flowers, fruit and vegetables — need these minerals to keep them healthy.

FLOWERS and FRUIT

Potash please!

LEAVES

I need nitrates!

ROOTS

Please feed me phosphates!

Part Three

CREATING A FERTILE SOIL

ORGANIC MATTER IS BEST

- Remember, organic gardeners feed the soil, not the plant, so it is important to give the soil plenty of organic matter - anything that has been alive and has rotted down.

- The best complete plant food is well-rotted manure or compost.

- If the manure has been mixed with wood shavings, don't dig it in but use it instead as a mulch around trees and shrubs.

- Pigeon and poultry manure are very strong and should be put in the compost heap. Avoid manure from battery units; it can be toxic.

- Use a green manure when possible. (See page 29.)

- Sewage sludge is sometimes available but, as a precaution, use only on non-food plants.

- Leaf mould is an excellent source of humus, containing a little plant nutrient. (See page 24.)

- Seaweed is a whole food, complete with humus. If you live near the sea, pile it round your vegetables. But seaweed is very susceptible to radioactivity, so check first.

- Spent mushroom compost is good but nowadays can be a highly chemical, synthetic substance; so make sure it is organic.

- Worm compost is very rich and easily made, or it can be bought. It is best used as a mulch or in potting compost. (See page 25.)

- Excellent organic commercial preparations are now available.

- No need to dig - just spread the material thickly over the soil.

- Don't grow vegetables too near main roads as lead dust collects on the leaves and in the soil.

- Don't confuse garden compost with seed and potting compost, which is quite a different material and is dealt with later.

- The compost heap is the powerhouse of the garden, where all waste vegetation rots down to provide food for the next generation — a natural process but speeded up.

- The compost bin should be made of good insulating material, such as wood or brick. And keep it covered — a carpet is fine.

- Always site your heap directly onto the soil so that earthworms can complete the process once it has cooled.

- Place bricks or rolls of netting at the base for ventilation and start with coarse material, such as cabbage stalks or prunings.

- Put 20 cms of well mixed vegetation on this, covering it with a thin layer of manure or any organic activator. (See Page 23.)

- Next comes another 20 cms of material, followed by a sprinkling of lime or wood ash.

- Repeat these layers until the container is full, then cover it with a lid or carpet.

- A perfectly made compost heap should heat up to at least 60°c (140°f) in the first few days, killing weed seeds and many diseases. But to do this you must store the materials first, then make the heap in one go.

- However, most people find it more convenient to add a little bit by bit. This is fine but try to exclude seeds.

- A good compromise is to start with a small container, then transfer the contents to the larger heap when cool and shrunk.

INSIDE THE COMPOST HEAP

- You can compost almost anything which has lived, including hay, straw, bracken, tea leaves, moss, household waste, weeds, lawn mowings, old woollens, feathers, woollen carpets, hair, eggshells, rhubarb leaves, paper and soft prunings.

- Collect left-over products from the greengrocer.

- You can safely use up to 10% newspaper, soaked and shredded.

- Always mix coarse and fine materials well, or in thin layers, e.g. cabbage leaves with mowings. Shredding coarse materials makes them rot down more quickly.

- Avoid wood, autumn leaves, man-made materials, metals, roots of perennial weeds, diseased plants, cooked food and meat. The last two encourage rats.

- Make sure your woollens and carpets **are** wool and not synthetic, as these will never rot down. For the same reason, don't use the contents of your vacuum cleaner.

- A variety of weeds and wild flowers added to the compost will make it richer in vitamins and minerals.

- To revive a dried-up heap, turn it and add liquid activator. (See overleaf.) If too wet add shredded paper and remove the cover (in dry weather). Carpet is better than a plastic cover.

- Compost can be made without a container. Merely pile it on the ground and cover it, or put it in a trench.

- If you use a container of netting or wooden slats line it with cardboard or thick newspaper for insulation.

- A well-made compost heap which gets really hot will destroy 80% of chemical pesticides.

- See overleaf for details of activators.

ALL ABOUT ACTIVATORS

- An activator is any nitrogen-rich material added to the compost to speed up the decaying process and feed the bacteria which actually do the work of decomposition.

- Having so much of their favourite food means that they work faster and increase in numbers, making the decaying material hot enough to kill weed seeds and diseases.

- Grass mowings, comfrey or any soft greens such as weeds, are rich in nitrogen and ideal for the job.

- Unrotted manure makes an excellent activator, especially pigeon manure. Apply a 5 cms layer of manure for every 20 cms of waste, 2.5 cms for pigeon manure. Add gypsum to stored manure to prevent the smell.

- Animal manures added to compost are thought to convey extra disease resistance.

- Urine makes a good activator, diluted 3 to 1 with water.

- Alternatively, you could use a thin layer of dried blood or hoof and horn, although these are rather expensive as activators.

- If you have nothing else, add a thin sprinkling of soil but too much keeps the heap cold.

- A vegetarian alternative is seaweed meal at 135 grams per square metre of surface area but, again, this is an expensive way to use it.

- Commercial activators are available from organic suppliers.

- As a bonus, well-made compost will contain up to 25% more nitrate than was originally applied in the first place. This comes from the nitrogen in the air, captured by happy bacteria!

LEAF MOULD

- Rotted-down leaves produce a peat-like substance known as leaf mould, traditionally used as a growing medium.

- Unaccountably, it has been neglected in recent years since peat has been available commercially.

- Simply collect leaves each Autumn and put them somewhere to rot down. A netting 'cage', or plastic bags, will keep them together.

- They don't need an activator, heat or air, just a little moisture. Press them down and leave.

- After a year they will have decomposed sufficiently to use as a mulch around trees and shrubs.

- In two years they will produce a superb, friable compost that is in every way a substitute for peat.

- It is very suitable for seed and potting compost when sieved. Being free from disease or weed seeds no sterilising is needed.

- This means that you have the advantage of live compost, which gives the plants a head start.

- Leaf mould contains only a small amount of plant food but is a rich source of humus. Earthworms will take it underground to enrich the soil.

- Avoid using leaves from main roads; they may be covered with lead dust.

- Its greatest asset is that it is a renewable resource - no landscape has been destroyed to obtain it.

- And it's free!

WORM COMPOST

- This system converts kitchen scraps and garden waste into a rich compost, ideal for a small garden or even no garden.

- The worms used are not earthworms but red brandlings used by fishermen. They can be found under damp surfaces in the garden or bought at angling shops.

- Any container can be used but an ordinary plastic dustbin with a well-fitting lid is quite suitable.

- Drill a few drainage holes about 15 cms from the base of the bin.

- Fill the bin with sand to a depth of about 20 cms and water this well. Cover with cardboard or wood cut to shape.

- On top of this comes the bedding - a few inches of peat substitute, leaf mould or old potting compost, for instance.

- Your bin is now ready to receive the worms, about 100 of which should be placed on the bedding. A layer of waste is now added.

- You can use almost anything organic - much more so than in a normal compost heap - meat, fish, bread, cooked food.

- As the worms slowly work their way through this material, keep adding further layers.

- When the compost is ready the worms and eggs go to start on the new batch.

- Worm compost is too rich to use neat but makes nutritious mulch or a component of potting compost.

- Fuller details are available in an HDRA leaflet. (See page 62.)

SMALL-SCALE WORM COMPOSTING

- The typical dustbin-size worm bin does not suit everyone. Removing the end product can be heavy work, or you may not have enough waste to fill it.

- In this case, you can use almost any size container which has a well-fitting lid.

- A polystyrene fish box is ideal for people without a garden who still want to recycle waste for use in containers.

- Make a few holes in the base and line it with damp newspaper.

- Place about 10 cms of bedding on this. Soil, old potting compost or peat substitute is suitable.

- Mix in a little dolomite or calcified seaweed to prevent acidity.

- Bedding in a small box will dry out more quickly, so it must be kept moist at all times.

- Put the worms (see previous page) on the bedding, cover with some sheets of damp newspaper and leave for a few days to settle.

- Add any kitchen waste mentioned on the previous page but place it to one side at first.

- When this has been converted into compost use the other side.

- After this, you should be able to apply the material over the whole surface.

- A great advantage of this size container is its mobility. It can easily be moved out of the hot sun, or into a shed for the Winter.

ORGANIC FERTILISERS

- There are several organic fertilisers available for those times when an extra mineral feed is needed.

- However, these are not pure chemicals but natural compounds which just happen to be rich in one particular mineral.

- They don't feed the plant immediately but decompose only slowly, releasing the minerals when needed.

- **Nitrates**: Dried blood is quick acting, although not now used by organic farmers because it is too soluble. Hoof and horn takes a few weeks to break down.

- **Phosphates**: Rock phosphate is a ground-up, natural rock. Bone meal is a renewable resource.

- **Potash**: Rock potash is a natural rock. Comfrey liquid or leaves are a renewable resource. (See next page.)

- **Calcium**: Ground limestone has a slower release than lime. Dolomite is approximately half calcium and half magnesium. Calcified seaweed is renewable and an excellent soil conditioner, with a wide range of trace elements but no nitrates.

- **All-round fertilisers**: Seaweed meal is one of the best. Apply three months in advance and lightly rake in.

- **General fertilisers**: Blood, fish and bone - but may contain chemical potash; or 3 parts dried blood, 6 parts bone meal and 8 parts seaweed meal; apply 110-170 grams per square metre.

- Some of the above are only obtainable from organic suppliers. (See page 62.)

COMFREY IN THE ORGANIC GARDEN

- Comfrey, a perennial herb, is invaluable for the organic gardener.

- It is rich in all nutrients, especially potash. To use the leaves, cut down to 5 cms, with at least three cuts a year.

- Make a high potash fertiliser by putting the leaves in a container weighed down with a brick and leaving for 3 to 4 weeks. Dilute the resulting black liquid with about 20 parts of water.

- Alternatively, soak leaves for 3 to 4 weeks in water and use neat, but the smell is powerful!

- The leaves can also be used as a nutritious mulch around the base of the plants, breaking down rapidly.

- Placed thickly in the potato trench it will produce superb results. Leave 24 hours before planting to let the leaves wilt.

- Start tomatoes off with compost/soil but, once fruiting begins, feed with comfrey liqud twice a week.

- Regular spraying with comfrey liquid improves a crop's health.

- It makes a good seed or potting compost, using half comfrey and half peat substitute, then left to rot down over the Winter.

- Comfrey is easily grown, its only disease being rust which can be cured by applying wood ash.

- Feed it with manure every Spring, preferably pigeon manure, obtainable free from pigeon fanciers.

- The roots go down very deep; so once planted it's hard to remove.

- It is easily propagated by means of root cuttings or offsets. Plant 60 cms apart.

- Comfrey is also a food, drink, animal fodder and medicinal plant.

GREEN MANURES

- A green manure is a plant grown purely to improve the soil, a method used traditionally by farmers.

- Any ground that is temporarily unused will soon be covered with weeds, so it's better to grow a plant of your own choosing.

- In Winter, a green manure prevents nutrients being washed out of bare soil and protects it against harsh weather conditions.

- When you need the ground again, lightly dig the plants in. Allow about a week for them to decompose - longer if sowing seeds.

- At the young, sappy stage the decomposing plants will enrich the soil with minerals and humus. So don't leave them to get tough and woody.

- If legumes are chosen, your soil will benefit from the additional nitrate. (See page 32.)

- Some green manures, such as phacelia or buckwheat, have attractive flowers which are a magnet for friendly insects.

- Green manures must be chosen with care to suit the needs of a particular growing scheme. They may be composed of either annuals or perennials.

- Some will be killed by the first frosts, so saving labour, while perennials like alfalfa can be over-wintered, providing several cuts for the compost heap.

- The commonest plants used as a green manure include grazing rye, trefoil, winter tares, mustard and clover.

- Fuller details can be found in an HDRA leaflet.

MORE SOURCES OF FERTILITY

- Nothing is ever wasted in the organic garden: almost everything organic can be recycled in some way.

- Wood ash from a bonfire is a good source of soluble potash; young twigs produce the most potash.

- Feathers are a very rich source of long-term nitrogen. Just tip them into a trench, 30 cms deep, and cover them with 20 cms of soil. This is ideal for all soft fruit but too rich for brassicas.

- Human hair, obtainable from the hairdresser, is also a useful source of long-term nitrogen.

- Tea leaves should never be thrown away. They contain slow-release nitrogen and the roses will appreciate them, as well as indoor plants. Cold tea contains potash.

- Soot is an old-fashioned fertiliser containing a little nitrogen, which helps to warm the soil and deter slugs.

- Nettles make a good liquid fertiliser. Soak in water and use the liquid.

- Any organic mulch will improve the soil. Shredded prunings, bark or sawdust are all suitable round shrubs and trees.

- Acid-loving plants will appreciate tea leaves, leaf mould, bracken and shredded pine needles.

- Foliar feeds are helpful when a plant needs a tonic. Use comfrey liquid or seaweed extract and spray the leaves.

- Perennial weeds, such as dock, bindweed and couch, if soaked in water for several weeks, produce a nutritious liquid feed.

A thick organic mulch with cold tea
      —just what your plants need.

SUMMARY OF ORGANIC FERTILISERS

MINERALS	FERTILISERS	OTHER SOURCES
NITRATES	Dried blood, hoof and horn.	Nettles, fish meal, soot, feathers, tea leaves, urine, legumes.
PHOSPHATE	Rock phosphate, bone meal.	Leaf mould, fish meal.
POTASH	Rock potash, comfrey.	Wood ash, nettles, cold tea, leaf mould, urine, young bracken.
CALCIUM	Ground limestone, calcified seaweed, dolomite.	Gypsum.
MAGNESIUM	Dolomite	Epsom salts (to correct deficiency only)
BORON	Borax (to correct deficiency only)	
TRACE ELEMENTS	Calcified seaweed, seaweed meal, liquid seaweed, comfrey.	

MAINTAINING FERTILITY

- Once you have achieved a really rich, fertile soil you must keep it like this to satisfy hungry plants.

- Regular applications of manure or compost are, of course, the main ingredient.

- Crop rotation is extremely important, giving the ground time to recover from each crop's action. (See page 35.)

- All plants of the legume family (peas and beans) have bacteria in their roots which manufacture their own nitrates from the air.

- This is why organic farmers don't need to buy nitrates - they grow legumes such as clover and plough them in.

- When peas and beans have been harvested leave the roots and a short stem. The extra nitrate will enrich the soil.

- Grow a green manure in the Winter, on temporarily spare ground, and dig it in while young and sappy. This prevents nutrients washing away and feeds the soil. (See page 29.)

- Nature always covers bare soil quickly, so using green manures means adopting nature's ideas and improving on them.

- Avoid walking on the soil as plants cannot grow in compacted earth. It is a good idea to make permanent pathways in your vegetable plot; this saves compost too.

- Raised beds mean extra fertility and better texture; plants can be grown much closer together, with higher yields.

- Mulching with organic materials raises fertility and improves soil structure as the worms get busy; so use any of the materials mentioned on the next page.

MULCHING

- A mulch is any material spread over the soil. It has many uses.

- Gardeners have traditionally mulched plants with compost or manure to feed the soil, as well as helping to retain moisture

- The ground must be thoroughly wet beforehand, as dry soil will remain dry and the plants will suffer.

- The mulch is a protection against drying winds, heavy rain, frost — in fact, an all-weather protection.

- The many insects flourishing under the mulch in this damp, dark and fertile atmosphere provide food for frogs, hedgehogs and other friendly creatures.

- It is an ideal habitat for beetles, which eat enormous numbers of slugs and other pests.

- Almost any organic material is suitable, such as hay, straw, leaf mould, bracken, lawn mowings, shredded pine needles, coir and other peat substitutes.

- The worms pull the mulch down and convert it into humus and compost, aerating and conditioning the soil as they go.

- Shredded wood products, such as bark, prunings or sawdust, would rob the soil of nitrogen if dug in but make an ideal mulch round shrubs and trees, where they will slowly decompose.

- If the mulch is thick enough (about 10 cms) it will help prevent annual weeds from germinating.

- Black plastic, carpet and similar mulches, while not feeding the soil, still provide many benefits. (See next page.)

MORE ABOUT MULCHES

- All plants need light to live, so the use of light-proof materials, such as black plastic or synthetic carpet means no weeds.

- Newspaper, cardboard and woollen carpets are also good but, being of organic origin, will rot down after one or two seasons.

- So, to clean up a weedy patch, or convert a lawn to a bed, just cover with carpet or black plastic and leave — best done in Spring.

- In a few months all annual weeds will have disappeared, but perennial weeds take much longer.

- The decaying weeds will feed the soil, which should now be clean enough for sowing and planting.

- But there's no need to wait for months. Make slits in the plastic and plant strong plants, adding compost, and disguise the ugly mulch with bark or chippings.

- A straw mulch is often used to keep strawberries clean but commercial growers now use woven black plastic, which suppresses weeds whilst letting the rain through.

- An excellent mulch for fruit trees is newspaper covered with lawn mowings (for nitrogen) topped up from time to time.

- Large stones or cobbles make an ornamental mulch. They attract heat and never blow away!

- Some people mulch the vegetable garden with waste vegetation instead of composting it — known as sheet composting. It rots down slowly but looks rather unattractive.

- A mulch of comfrey leaves round tomato or other plants produces an instant high potash feed.

CROP ROTATION

- Never grow the same crops continuously on the same ground, to prevent exhaustion of minerals and to allow the soil to recover.

- Root crops feed heavily on phosphates; brassicas are greedy for nitrates; peas need extra potash. Moving them round spreads the load.

- A four-year rotation, as shown below, is good, but pick one that suits you. You may prefer the onion family, for example, rather than one of the others.

- The plant families are moved round clockwise each year, fitting in other crops where space is available.

- When planning your rotation, remember the following points:

    Brassicas (cabbage family) can suffer from clubroot, so wait at least four years before returning them to the same ground.

    Lime the brassica bed the Autumn before planting to deter clubroot.

    Potatoes must not have lime as this encourages scab.

    Let leafy vegetables follow legumes to take advantage of extra nitrogen.

    Never use fresh manure on root crops.

    Potatoes are the grossest feeders and usually have any compost or manure if only a limited amount is available.

SEED AND POTTING COMPOST

- Gardeners traditionally used to mix a different compost for each plant, using sieved leaf mould as a base.

- Organic mixtures are available commercially but it's easier, and cheaper, to make your own. (It's not necessary to have the same precisely standardised product as a commercial grower.)

- We prefer not to use peat so that our few remaining peat bogs are preserved, but there are plenty of alternatives based on recycled waste, the best being leaf mould. (See page 24.)

- John Innes mixtures are tried and tested and an organic mixture based on these is ideal.

- Seed Compost (JI no. 1): 2 parts loam or good garden soil, 1 part sieved leaf mould or peat substitute and 1 part sharp sand, with 50 grams each of bone meal and calcified seaweed per bucket.

- Potting Compost (JI no. 2): 7 parts loam, 3 parts leaf mould, 2 parts silver sand, with 100 grams of general fertiliser per bucket. (See page 27.)

- A popular, all-purpose compost is comfrey leaf mould, made by leaving alternate layers of comfrey and leaf mould to rot down over the Winter. Add 1 part sharp sand to 4 parts final mixture.

- Compost for container plants needs to be richer, an ideal mix being 1 part worm compost, 1 part garden compost, 1 part leaf mould, 1 part sharp sand, with 50 grams of calcified seaweed per bucket.

- However, it's interesting to experiment using different materials. I often convert seed compost into potting compost merely by adding hoof and horn or garden compost.

- When using leaf mould as a base, remember that it not only absorbs water more easily than peat but also dries out faster.

Part Four

FIGHTING PESTS
AND DISEASES

THE STORY OF INSECTS

- Know your enemy - and your friends.

- Insects go through four distinct stages, varying in length according to weather conditions.

Adult

The adult insect usually lays its eggs on one particular plant family only, seeking it by sight and scent. It needs nectar to live.

Eggs

Look for eggs on underside of leaf and crush them before they can hatch.

Caterpillar

Caterpillar (grub, larva) spends its time feeding. This is when most damage is done. Remove by hand if possible. Caterpillars provide food for many predators, including wasps and birds.

Pupa

Pupa (chrysalis) lies dormant in soil or bark until conditions are right, when it sheds its skin and emerges as an adult. Birds and beetles eat most of them.

THE FIRST LINE OF DEFENCE

- Prevention is always best, and most organic methods are ways of preventing the pest from reaching the plant.

- A healthy plant can resist attack; enemies always go for the weakest.

- There is no need for wholesale extermination of all insect life, just control. We can spare a leaf or two!

- Choose plants that are resistant to their particular disease: for instance, potatoes which are resistant to eelworm and roses which are resistant to blackspot.

- Grow the plant in the kind of situation it enjoys: for example, a shade-loving plant will not thrive in full sun.

- Move the plants round the plot. (See page 35.) Crop rotation prevents a build-up of soil pests.

- Encourage predators - the natural enemies of the pest and the gardener's friends. (See next page.)

- Use physical barriers to prevent the fly from reaching your plant. (See page 42.)

- Timing sometimes helps; sow carrot seeds when the carrot fly is laying her eggs, late May/early June or late July/early August.

- Avoid monoculture; cottage gardeners always grew their cabbages amongst the flowers to confuse the pests.

- Many people use companion planting; some plants thrive when grown together. Strong-smelling herbs planted in the vegetable plot can fool flying pests.

- Garden hygiene is important. Remove all decayed leaves and destroy diseased materials.

ENCOURAGING PREDATORS

- A flock of birds on the lawn, ladybirds, beetles and other wildlife in the garden, are all busy accounting for millions of pests daily. We CANNOT do without them so don't kill them with chemicals.

- The most important thing you can do to encourage predators is to banish all chemicals, providing a safe environment.

- Organic pest control, in fact, depends on a good balance of both pests and predators.

- Make room somewhere for a few weeds, in other words wild flowers. These will provide a habitat for many predators as well as a home for friendly, pest-eating insects.

- Build a pond - a small one will do - and bring in frogspawn and toadspawn. Frogs and toads eat vast quantities of unfriendly insects and slugs.

- Encourage hedgehogs; these will dispose of many pests.

- Grow the kind of plants that attract hoverflies, such as marigold and poached egg plant. Hoverfly larvae account for many aphids.

- Birds are greedy for insects in all their stages, so attract them with bird boxes and tables, and grow berried plants. Seed heads left on plants throughout the winter are an important source of food at a difficult time of year for birds.

- Hang pieces of fat in apple and rose trees. Birds will come for the fat and take caterpillars and pupae while there.

- A flock of free range hens pecking round fruit trees will dispose of codling moth and other unwanted pupae.

- The best slug remover, undoubtedly, is a couple of ducks.

THE WILDLIFE GARDEN

- A wide variety of wildlife is the best guarantee of pest control, providing a natural balance between pests and predators.

- Above all, wild creatures need an undisturbed area — not easy in a small, tidy garden but still possible.

- For instance, the spaces behind mature trees and shrubs can be left untouched, just adding twigs and prunings occasionally. Such an area makes an ideal habitat for hedgehogs.

- Throwing weeds behind the hedge will increase the earthworm population, which provides food for birds and other predators.

- Plant a shady border with a permanent succession of spring flowers, such as snowdrops and bluebells, to be followed by ferns.

- The ferns disguise the yellowing leaves. Such a border can remain untouched and weedfree for years, and is also very attractive.

- Ivy on fences and walls provides nesting sites for birds.

- Stock your garden with plants which attract bees, butterflies and other insects. A herb garden is an insect's paradise.

- Native British flowers and trees are preferable to exotic species as insects and small creatures prefer them and are adapted to them.

- Many modern hybrids are sterile or have inaccessible pollen. Often, the more showy the flower, the less interest for bees.

- Birds, frogs and other creatures will come to eat the insects and dispose of pests while they're there.

- A wildflower lawn is an attractive and beneficial feature, but must be carefully planted and maintained.

- For more information read *Gardening for Wildlife*. (See page 63.)

PEST BARRIERS

- Barriers of different kinds are ideal to keep out the flying pest that is looking for somewhere to lay her eggs. Once the grub is hatched, the problem is much more difficult.

- Probably the best barrier is netting of the correct mesh size, ranging from very fine spun nylon to a fruit cage against birds.

- Covering cabbages and other plants with fine mesh from the earliest stages will keep out aphids, butterflies and several other pests.

- Many people grow carrots, lettuces and other vulnerable plants in cold frames or polytunnels to keep out pests.

- A square of underfelt around the plant is very efficient at keeping out cabbage root fly. It also has the advantage of harbouring beetles, one of the most useful predators in the garden.

- An upturned yoghurt carton with a hole burnt in the base, put firmly round young plants, keeps out root flies, cabbage moth and the cutworm.

- A polythene or fine mesh 'fence', about 60 cms high, erected around a row of carrots will deter carrot flies, which never fly above this height. Carrots flourish in the extra shelter.

- Sprinkle gritty material around plants to deter slugs and snails.

- Sections of plastic bottles pressed in around vulnerable plants will keep out slugs and some other soil-borne pests.

- Insect barrier glue protects plants against several pests, including vine weevil.

- See the *Organic Gardening Catalogue* for a selection of other barriers.

THE SLUG PROBLEM

- Undoubtedly, this is the most widespread problem in the garden, although slugs are useful scavengers.

- Slug pellets can damage or kill wildlife and pets.

- The best long term solution is to encourage predators but ducks are the most efficient. (See page 40.)

- Certain precautions will help, the main one being to keep the ground clean and free of decaying leaves, a slug's staple diet.

- However, some people believe that a mulch of mowings and decaying leaves keeps the slug happy and away from precious plants, but this will increase the slug population.

- Slugs dislike anything rough on their slimy bodies. So sprinkle grit, ashes, shredded bark, egg shells, soot or similar material round vulnerable plants. Some will need renewing after rain.

- A popular remedy is to sink a jar of weak beer in the soil at ground level. Slugs are attracted to this and drown. Unfortunately, so do friendly beetles. If this happens raise the level of the jar.

- One idea is a miniature electric 'fence' around the bed, which is a good idea as long as no slugs are within the enclosed area.

- The most effective protection of young plants is a section of plastic bottle pushed firmly into the ground around each plant, which also acts as a miniature greenhouse.

- Many people go slug-hunting at night with a torch; hundreds can be caught in this way. Pick them up with tweezers and drop them into a bowl of salty water. Alternatively, put damp newspapers on the ground and periodically remove slugs which collect underneath.

- A biological control now available is proving quite successful.

SNAILS

- Snails can be a much more difficult problem than slugs, as they generally climb and attack living plants. With their 135 rows of teeth, each containing 106 teeth, their effect can be devastating.

- Snails need calcium for their shells, so are not usually found in acidic soils, unless the garden wall or patio is alkaline.

- If you use ornamental chippings, avoid limestone, as this could attract snails into the garden.

- A layer of sharp sand around vulnerable plants is quite effective as a deterrent.

- If you're really desperate, shake a thin sprinkling of salt round the edge of the sand, replacing it after rain, but it may not suit the plant.

- Slugs can arch over a salt barrier but snails may find this more of a problem.

- They will climb up fences and other supports, so protect them too!

- A strip of coarse sandpaper round pots, containers and raised beds has proved to be quite effective.

- The natural enemy of snails is the thrush, but pesticides, loss of habitat and cats have decimated their numbers and there are now very few thrushes about.

- Snails seem to develop a liking for certain plants and sometimes it's wisest to admit defeat and just grow something else!

- However, a serious and determined snail hunt, especially at night with a torch, is probably the most long-lasting control, but seek out the tiny baby snails too, as they are prolific breeders.

- Snails love bran, so leave some around before your snail hunt.

YOU'VE GOT A PROBLEM?

- Despite all our efforts, there will still be some pests and diseases or the plants may not be developing correctly. So first find the cause of the trouble.

- Check that your cultivation techniques are correct for that plant: for instance sprouts like firm ground. And is the plant happy in its allotted position?

- You may have sown the seed too early before the soil has warmed, or it may have rotted or been eaten by mice. Every seed requires a different germination temperature.

- Constant inspection of plants will help to catch problems before they have a chance to become disasters.

- Remove pests by hand if possible. Look on the underside of leaves for eggs and caterpillars.

- Many apparent diseases are really signs of mineral deficiency. (See next page.)

- If your soil is deficient in one mineral, find out why. Has it been locked in by a too-generous application of some other mineral? (See page 47.)

- If you are unsure how to cure it, spray the leaves with liquid seaweed. This contains every mineral and the plant will take what it needs.

- Many tricks and traps exist for individual problems. (See the catalogues of organic organisations on page 61.)

- Observe good garden hygiene; remove dead leaves and branches, particularly if diseased.

- If all else fails use a spray but **only** an organic one. (See page 48.)

MINERAL DEFICIENCIES

Always look up the symptoms of mineral deficiency first before assuming that your plants have some terrible disease. Here are some of the commonest symptoms ...

Mineral Deficiency	Symptom	Short-term Cure	Long-term Cure
Nitrate	Pale, under-sized, poorly developed leaves.	Dried blood, hoof and horn.	Organic matter
Potash	Brown on the outer leaf edge, chocolate spot on broad beans.	Comfrey liquid or wood ash.	Rock Potash
Phosphate	Purple or blue-green tints on leaves.	Comfrey liquid or liquid seaweed spray.	Bone meal or rock phosphate
Magnesium	Yellowing leaves but veins stay green.	28 grams Epsom salts in 9 litres water, over 2 square metres, or as foliar feed.	Dolomite
Boron	Brown curd in cauliflower, brown rot in swedes.	1 teaspoon borax in 4.5 litres water over 6 square metres.	Calcified seaweed, seaweed meal.
Calcium	Blossom end rot in tomatoes.	Lime	Dolomite or calcified seaweed.

If you're not sure of the correct cure, spray with liquid seaweed.

WHAT'S LOCKED UP?

- It is extremely important that minerals are present in the soil in the right proportions to each other. If there is too much of one kind, others may become locked up and unobtainable. Too much trace element is as bad as too little.

- For this reason, approach soil testing with caution. There may be plenty of minerals in the soil but the plant cannot get at them.

- For example:

an overdose of:	leads to locking up of:
potash	boron and magnesium
lime (calcium)	boron, iron, manganese
nitrate	calcium and copper
magnesium	calcium
phosphate	zinc and potash

- Plants fed organically rarely suffer from locking up deficiencies or overdoses, because minerals in organic matter are present, naturally, in the right proportions.

ORGANIC SPRAYS

- Organic pesticides, made from either vegetable or animal substances, break down quickly in the soil, doing no lasting harm.

- Nevertheless, these sprays do kill insects, so use them only as a last resort and as late as possible in the evening when friendly insects have retired for the night.

- The best all-round spray is soft soap, which is effective for aphids and small caterpillars. Add it to other sprays as a wetting agent.

- Derris is very effective for many pests but kills beneficial insects, so use it sparingly. It breaks down in 48 hours.

- Pyrethrum is equally effective for many pests but breaks down in 12 hours.

- The best caterpillar spray is BT, which is a bacterium that is specific to caterpillars only. Several other biological controls are now becoming available.

- Burgundy and Bordeaux mixtures are fungicides which are permitted where no other remedy is available. Research is continuing to find a more environmentally-friendly fungicide.

- Quassia chips are excellent for sawfly.

- There are now several other commercial preparations which are safely organic, one of which is insecticidal soap.

- Many of these sprays can only be obtained from suppliers of organic materials. (See page 62.)

- **NB** Some organic sprays may contravene new regulations, so check first: for example, nicotine, the traditional remedy for sawfly, has been withdrawn from the market because of legislation.

SOME HOME-MADE REMEDIES

> The following traditional remedies can no longer be recommended because of EC legislation.

- The liquid from boiled-up rhubarb leaves makes an excellent aphid killer. Simmer 40 grams leaves in 1 litre water for $1/4$ hour, diluting with 3 parts water.

- Elder leaves boiled up similarly are equally effective and are also a mild fungicide, giving some protection against blackspot.

- Urine can be sprayed on fruit trees and is effective against scab - sprayed neat in January and diluted 3 to 1 before leaf fall.

- To eliminate ants, which protect aphids, mix equal parts icing sugar and borax; then sprinkle the mixture in their usual haunts.

- Bicarbonate of soda is quite an effective, mild fungicide for powdery mildew. Mix 2 teaspoons to 4.5 litres of water, add a little soft soap and spray twice a week.

- People used to boil up a brew of strong smelling herbs such as tansy or garlic, spraying it as a masking scent against flying pests.

- A pot of French marigolds in the greenhouse usually deters whitefly.

- Tagetes minuta has root secretions that can kill ground elder, bindweed and eelworm.

- Continued research is turning up new remedies and ideas for defeating pests and diseases. Yet old-fashioned ones still have their uses: for instance, permanganate of potash and washing soda were both popular at one time as fungicides.

WEED CONTROL

- There is no organic weedkiller but some weeds, which are only wild flowers, should be given some space somewhere in the garden to provide a habitat for friendly insects and other predators.

- Constant hoeing will prevent weeds getting a hold while plants are becoming established.

- Remember that plants can't live without light, so a light-proof mulch will prevent weeds from growing.

- Suitable materials are black polythene, cardboard, carpet or several thicknesses of newspaper. They can be disguised with chippings or shredded bark.

- Regular organic mulches will suppress annual weeds while feeding the soil.

- A way of cleaning the vegetable plot before sowing is to allow annual weeds to germinate on the seedbed first, removing them before sowing.

- Some people use a flame gun to burn weeds on path or plot. This is very effective but must be used with care.

- Discourage perennial weeds by constantly removing leaves and flowers. In a couple of years, they will give up.

- To get rid of perennial weeds in the lawn, an old pair of scissors or a knife will remove the root.

- Boiling water is very effective for spot-weeding.

- Perennial weeds in the flower bed can be removed by covering thickly with a loose organic material, so that the roots grow into it and can, in time, be easily lifted.

Part Five

ORGANIC EXTRA

THE HERB GARDEN

- There should always be a place in the organic garden for some herbs.

- Herbs are either native British flowers or Mediterranean imports.

- Concentrated aromatic oils give herbs their distinctive smell and taste.

- Their flowers are never large and showy but they act as a magnet to all insects.

- The insects attract birds and other wildlife, all helping to deal with pests.

- Herbs are useful for cooking, for medicine and for their aroma.

- Planted round the vegetable garden, herbs can keep off flying pests which hunt by scent. A boiled-up brew can have the same effect if used as a spray.

- Herbs like a dry situation in full sun and generally should never be fed with compost or manure, which makes them soft, lose their flavour and become susceptible to pests.

- Bone meal and calcified seaweed provide all the minerals herbs need, with leaf mould for humus.

- The only exceptions to this are chives and parsley, which appreciate some nitrogen in their feed.

- If your rosemary dies, the cause is almost always too rich soil.

- The herb garden needs very little maintenance, just a trim and tidy in the Autumn.

- Herbs can stand drought better than most other plants.

THE ORGANIC LAWN

- Lawn care is the same no matter what system you use, but, as with other plants, good husbandry is the key to success.

- Choose the right kind of grass for your purpose, coarse for hard wear, finer if you want a bowling green.

- If you can mow the lawn twice a week leave off the grass box. The fine mowings will feed the lawn, recycling the goodness you usually remove.

- For the occasional spring feed, use sieved compost or any other general purpose organic food. (See page 27.)

- For an Autumn top dressing, use ordinary garden soil mixed with a little sand, more on heavy soil.

- Weeds in the lawn can be a problem but many people actually like to see daisies and other wild flowers on the lawn.

- Regular mowing should keep the lawn free of weeds, but the roots of nuisances like dandelions can be removed by hand with a knife. Salt on the growing point is lethal to weeds.

- Moss is a sign of acidity, dampness, starvation or too much shade, and can often be cured by adding lime or ground limestone.

- Lime alone can make a remarkable improvement to a half-starved lawn, as the lime stimulates the nitrate-forming microbes in the soil to get busy.

- If you're not a 'bowling green' enthusiast and just want a healthy green lawn, sow seeds of dwarf white clover. (See page 62.)

- The clover, being a legume, will feed the lawn. It will stay green in a drought and, once established, you should never need to feed the lawn again!

THE ORGANIC GREENHOUSE

- The organic greenhouse requires exactly the same regime as an organic garden, which means using good, organic soil and practising crop rotation, but paying special attention to hygiene.

- The greenhouse can be used all year round to produce a huge variety of flowers and vegetables.

- Grow some flowers to attract beneficial insects. A resident toad will help to keep the place free of slugs and other pests.

- Grow a green manure in any empty space. (See page 29.) Being able to use a frost tender variety is an extra advantage.

- The main problem in such an enclosed space is fungal disease caused by damp and, as you will not be using a fungicide, extra care must be taken.

- Good ventilation is essential. Open the windows as much as possible and fit extra vents if necessary.

- Restrict watering in cold weather and leave this until the morning, taking care not to splash water on leaves.

- Water potted plants from below, standing them in about 2.5 cms of water until all the soil is soaked.

- Mulch the beds after watering to keep the beds dry. (See page 33.)

- An electric fan heater is excellent, ventilating and heating at the same time.

- A compost bin in the corner helps to keep the greenhouse warm in Winter, as the decomposing waste heats up.

- Some people have experimented with a solar greenhouse. Solar panels provide sustainable, non-polluting heat, which is free.

VARIATIONS ON AN ORGANIC THEME

- Many unusual, even eccentric, kinds of organic gardening exist as alternative methods.

- There is the Gertrude Franck system of companion planting which grows food through a living mulch.

- Another method is the Fukuoka system which believes in never turning over the soil.

- An adaptation of this method is to cover the soil with several layers of cardboard or newspaper, followed by a mulch of vegetable waste or mowings.

- After a few weeks of soaking in the rain, the mulch is pulled back and seeds sown onto the paper.

- Then there is the German Mound System, which consists of several layers of material, starting with a small, rounded pile of twigs or prunings.

- On this, in order, go inverted grass sods, dead leaves, a scattering of soil and, finally, a compost and soil mixture.

- Firm it gently down and cover with grass, straw or horse manure.

- This mound provides a warm, fertile base for earlier planting and lasts for about five years, occasionally being topped up with compost.

- There is also veganic gardening, which avoids all animal products and uses liquid feeds of seaweed, grass mowings and soot.

- Several other systems are promoted and tried from time to time with varying degrees of success. But the best known and most successful is biodynamic gardening. (See next page.)

BIODYNAMIC GARDENING

- This is a specialised from of organic gardening, based on the work of Rudolph Steiner.

- The aim of this method is to work in tune with the earth, guided by its natural rhythms and patterns.

- Planting is timed by the movement of sun, moon and stars.

- The time of day is also important for sowing, planting and harvesting.

- A special calendar is used by biodynamic gardeners, giving the precise day and time for planting and other activities.

- Leaf vegetables and herbs are picked in the morning, while root vegetables are harvested in the afternoon and evening.

- Diversity and variety of plants are very important so that they benefit from each other's presence.

- Special homeopathic substances are used at various stages of cultivation to stimulate the life forces.

- There are special rules about composting, adding homeopathic preparations, with a final layer of soil, mowings, straw and bracken to conserve moisture.

- Cultivation is done only in shallow soil, never deeper than 7.5 cms, while compost must not be dug in any deeper than this.

- There are several biodynamic farms, here and on the Continent, which sell food under the trade symbol of *Demeter*.

- For further information the address is on page 61.

Part Six

SUMMING UP

GETTING STARTED

- You've decided to go organic but don't know where to start?

First, put all your chemicals in the bin, then start a compost heap.

Get some manure; riding schools and farms often sell it cheaply.

- Use only well-rotted manure and make sure it's mixed with straw and not wood shavings.

- If you have no manure or compost, apply a general fertiliser. (See page 27.)

- Try to manage two applications of organic matter, one in Autumn, another in Spring. Apply it thickly to the soil's surface.

- Never leave the soil bare; either cover it up or sow a green manure. (See page 29.)

- Weeds allowed to grow over Winter provide nature's green manure but don't allow them to seed. Just hoe them off in Spring.

- If your soil is still impoverished or acid, calcified seaweed will perk it up.

- Don't expect your vegetables to be fully organic for two or three years if you have previously used chemicals. They will only gradually leach away.

- Grow attractant flowers near vegetables to attract bees, hoverflies and other beneficial insects. Herbs are a good idea too.

- You may get very poor results for a year or so until a proper balance has been established, but be patient and persevere. You won't regret it.

PEST AND DISEASE CONTROL
A Comparison of Different Methods

CHEMICAL	ORGANIC
Chemical sprays poison and kill the soil.	Sprays are harmless and enrich the soil.
Most pesticides kill all insects indiscriminately.	A wide variety of insects are encouraged.
Herbicides destroy wild flowers.	Wild flowers are an essential part of organic growing.
Handling pesticides endangers human health.	No danger, only healthy activity.
Residues in food cause ill health.	Organic food is good for you.
Chemicals fight and confront nature.	Organic methods respect and promote the natural world.
Biocides endanger the food chain.	All creatures proliferate in safety.
The balance of nature is destroyed.	The balance of nature is an integral part of pest control.
The whole environment is polluted - air, land and water.	It conserves and improves the environment.
Chemicals are expensive to buy.	Many organic methods involve no cost at all except physical effort.

Are you creating an environmentally hazardous zone?

FEEDING THE PLANT
A Comparison of Different Methods

CHEMICAL	ORGANIC
Immediate take-up by plant.	Slow release - only taken up when required.
Usually causes overdose of nitrates.	Plant takes the amount it needs and no more.
Often deficient in trace elements.	Supplies full range of minerals and trace elements.
Interferes with and upsets natural processes.	Reinforces nature's bio-system.
Earthworms either killed or deterred.	Earthworms multiply rapidly in this favourable habitat.
Uses up the earth's supply of non-renewable resources.	As few renewables used as possible.
Encourages shallow rooting.	Leads to deep roots and good healthy root system.
Slowly destroys the humus.	Develops and maintains humus.
Toxic minerals easily absorbed.	Mainly filters out harmful elements.
Pollutes water, encourages algae.	Conserves the natural environment.
Very expensive to buy.	Many materials are free and involve recycling what would otherwise be garbage.

ORGANIC ORGANISATIONS

Henry Doubleday Research Association,
National Centre for Organic Gardening,
Ryton-on-Dunsmore, Coventry, CV8 3LG
Telephone: 01203 303517

Soil Association,
Bristol House, Victoria Street, Bristol, BS1 6DF
Telephone: 0117 9290 661

WWOOF (Working Weekends on Organic Farms),
19 Bradford Road, Lewes, E. Sussex, BN7 1RB

Biodynamic Agricultural Association,
Woodman Lane, Clent, Stourbridge, West Midlands, DY9 9PX
Telephone: 01562 884933

Good Gardeners' Association,
Pinetum Lodge, Churcham, Gloucester, GL2 8AD
Telephone: 01452 750402

Centre for Alternative Technology,
Machynlleth, Powys, SY20 9AZ
Telephone: 01654 702400

ORGANIC SUPPLIERS

Henry Doubleday Research Association,
National Centre for Organic Gardening,
Ryton-on-Dunsmore, Coventry, CV8 3LG
Telephone: 01203 303517
Seeds, gardening products, books, food and gifts. (Personal customers only.)

Soil Association,
Bristol House, Victoria Street, Bristol, BS1 6DF
Telephone: 0117 9290661
Books and gifts.

John Chambers,
15 Westleigh Road, Barton, Seagrove, Kettering,
Northants, NN15 5AJ
Telephone: 01933 652562
Suppliers of wildflower seeds.

Chase Organics (GB) Ltd,
River Dene Estate, Molesey Road, Hersham, Surrey, KT12 4RG
Telephone: 01932 253666   *Fax:* 01932 252707
Seeds, gardening products and books. They also publish an organic gardening catalogue.

FURTHER READING

Organic Gardening by L D Hills

A Month by Month Guide to Organic Gardening by L D Hills

Companion Planting - Successful Gardening the Organic Way
by Gertrude Franck

RHS Organic Gardening by Pauline Pears and Sue Stickland

The Complete Manual of Organic Gardening
edited by Basil Caplan

Successful Organic Gardening by Geoff Hamilton

The Gardening from Which? Guide to Gardening Without Chemicals by The Consumers Association

Gardening for Wildlife by George Pilkington
In this series, the companion book to *Organic Gardening*.

The Henry Doubleday Research Association has a large selection of books and pamphlets dealing with specific topics.

ABOUT THE AUTHOR

- Ruth Jacobs has been an organic gardener for over thirty years. She started *Liverpool Organic Gardeners* in 1984 and was its secretary until 1998. She is a freelance writer and has edited their magazine for many years.

- This book has been written for the many puzzled gardeners Ruth meets who want to know more about organic growing. Based on the notes and handouts she used when lecturing for the WEA, it aims to answer some of the many queries she still receives.

- Ruth is on the writing team of the magazine, *Organic Gardening* - an essential buy for all enthusiasts - and has appeared on TV's Channel 4 in the *All Muck and Magic* series.

- Ruth lives with her husband on the outskirts of Liverpool, where her garden abounds with wild flowers, herbs, vegetables and fruit - all organically grown, of course!